PATHWAY   JUL   1 8

SO-AHV-716

GAYLORD   PRINTED IN U.S.A.

Rewarding Trips
In and Around Deerfield

By David J. McLaughlin and Laren Bright

Photographs by
Jim McElholm and David J. McLaughlin
©2006

Pentacle Press

Valley: *Rewarding Trips In and Around Deerfield*

First print edition 2006

No part of this publication may be reproduced by any mechanical, photographic or electronic process or in the form of a photographic recording, nor may it be stored in a retrieval system, transmitted or otherwise copied for public or private use without prior written permission from the publisher.

Library of Congress Control Number: 2005900746

ISBN 0-9763500-1-7

SAN 255-4860

For further information on this publication and related Pathways to the Past products, visit our website at www.pentacle-press.com.

To contact the publisher write:

Pentacle Press
P.O. Box 9400
Scottsdale, AZ 85252

Printed in Hong Kong

GETTING THE MOST FROM THIS GUIDE

The Upper Pioneer Valley is a 20th century term that refers to the small towns spread out along the Connecticut River in the upper half of western Massachusetts.

At the historic center of this fertile area, first settled in the middle of the 17th century, is the town of Deerfield, a beleaguered frontier outpost during the French and Indian Wars (1689-1763). Deerfield is a living museum of New England history and art. However, many who flock to Deerfield only see part of its historic legacy. Even fewer know where to look to find other well-preserved towns and villages and other significant attractions in the Upper Pioneer Valley. The crowded access roads to Deerfield (US 91 and Route 5) do not invite further exploration.

This guide has been organized to show you the most compelling attractions in Old Deerfield and to present a variety of lesser-known attractions along the back country roads to the east and west of Deerfield.

At the back of the guide are listings of resources, places to stay and references. Consult them to help you plan your trip, and keep in mind the following tips:

Many of the towns just south of the journeys we outline are bustling college towns (Amherst, South Hadley, Northampton). They offer good accommodations, excellent restaurants … and a lot of traffic.

Be sure you have a detailed map (the spiralbound Arrow and JIMAPCO Western Massachusetts Maps are good choices). While we show you all the important routes, this is an area made for wandering back country roads, and maps that show all the town roads are essential.

Check for festivals, craft shows, concerts and other special activities using the Internet links and phone numbers provided.

All in all, we hope you find *Exploring the Upper Pioneer Valley* both a useful resource in planning and navigating your trip and a wonderful visual memento of this unique part of our country.

TABLE OF
Contents

Pioneer Valley Beginnings	6
The Preservation of Deerfield	12
Deerfield Today	18
South Deerfield	30
Whately	34
Sunderland	38
Hadley	42
Leverett	47
Montague Center	56
Lake Pleasant	64
On to Conway	66
Conway	68
Ashfield	76
Plainfield	82
Cummington	86
Goshen	90
Williamsburg	98
Things to Consider	100
Accommodations	102
Supplemental Reading	104
Useful Contacts	105
Photography Credits	106
Acknowledgments	108
About the Authors and Photographers	109
Index	110

LEFT: HISTORIC DEERFIELD HOUSE

6

PIONEER VALLEY
Beginnings

Visiting the Upper Pioneer Valley takes us back in time to the frontier of colonial New England in the second half of the 17th century and touches upon the days of the very earliest colonial settlers. A brief excursion through the history of the area will enrich your experience of the towns you encounter.

When the *Mayflower* landed at Plymouth in 1620, the Pilgrims were ill prepared for the harsh New England weather. They had intended to join other settlers who, in 1607, had established a colony in Virginia, where the climate was more hospitable. But weather and other factors changed their well-intentioned plans.

PILGRIMS LANDING 1620

PILGRIMS BEING GREETED

As we learned in grade school, an Indian chief of the Wampanoag tribe, Massasoit, brought food to sustain the settlers during their first winter.

For some years relations between the Native Americans and the English settlers were friendly. However, as more and more colonists arrived, the situation deteriorated.

Settlements quickly spread beyond Plymouth. About 1,000 Puritans settled Salem in 1630, led by John Winthrop, who founded the Massachusetts Bay Colony. Rhode Island was founded in 1636, New Hampshire in 1639.

One of the most desirable areas to settle was the rich delta surrounding the Connecticut River, because it was ideal for farming. Even today the river snakes through an Upper Pioneer Valley countryside near Deerfield, rich with family farms and plenty of open spaces.

William Pynchon, an ambitious Puritan businessman, purchased land from the Agawam nation and founded Springfield in 1636. His son John extended settlements north, founding Northampton in 1653.

CONNECTICUT RIVER NEAR DEERFIELD, MASSACHUSETTS

KING PHILIP

PREPARING FOR CONFLICT

By 1669 a town named Pocumtuck had been established further up the Connecticut River. The smaller village of Northfield was settled two years later, in 1671.

Even with a burgeoning settlement population, the Upper Pioneer Valley remained a dangerous frontier in the 17th century. Indian attacks were not uncommon.

In 1675 fighting broke out on a wide front, starting in southeastern Massachusetts. The leader who initiated attacks was Metacomet, the son of the Indian Chief Massasoit, who had been so helpful to the Pilgrims some fifty-five years earlier.

The English called Metacomet "King" Philip, and this bloody conflict is referred to as King Philip's War. The uprisings spread spontaneously all along the frontier. The towns organized militia and stepped up training.

Even so, the frontier settlements were still quite vulnerable. During almost two years of continuous conflict, fifty-two of the ninety towns that existed in Puritan New England were attacked, and thirteen of them were destroyed.

One of the towns that was hardest hit was Pocumtuck, which by then had a population of 200. In the fall of 1675, as the danger of an Indian attack increased, the town's women and children were sent away to safer locations further down the valley, leaving fifty men to try to hold the town. They were quickly reinforced with a large contingent of soldiers from Hadley, where a garrison was stationed.

On the morning of September 18, 1675, a wagon train loaded with threshed wheat set out from Pocumtuck, guarded by 80 soldiers under the command of Captain Thomas Lathrop. The

ATTACK AT BLOODY BROOK   DEATH OF PHILIP

convoy was attacked by hundreds of King Philip's warriors as they crossed a stream later renamed Bloody Brook.

Only eight soldiers survived. Pocumtuck was abandoned shortly afterward and then totally destroyed by Philip's warriors. The settlement was reestablished after Philip was killed in an ambush in 1676.

By 1680 the rebuilt town – renamed Deerfield – had grown to 260 people. A few peaceful years were soon followed by decades of conflict as a series of colonial wars between the French and English kept the frontier a caldron and discouraged any expansion further up the valley.

Deerfield was attacked again on Februrary 29, 1704, by a group of Indians led by the French. By the time the battle was finished, forty-eight settlers had been killed and 111 inhabitants carted off to Canada. The captives included the Reverend John Williams, the town pastor, two of whose children were massacred and whose wife was captured and then killed on the outskirts of present-day Greenfield because she was physically unable keep up.

Deerfield, resettled in 1707, remained a frontier outpost for over fifty years.

1704 ATTACK ON DEERFIELD

THE PRESERVATION OF
Deerfield

COMMEMORATING DEERFIELD

The town emerged from these dark years with a rich history that guaranteed the interest of subsequent generations.

What makes Deerfield special, however, is that several unique factors united to make this one of the best-preserved historic towns in all of New England.

The town itself was laid out with homes clustered around a long, wide thoroughfare (still just called "The Street"), with farm plots extending out in wide strips on either side.

Much of the original town land continued to be farmed well into the 20th century. The citizens of Old Deerfield also had the wisdom to preserve its handsome common.

A VIEW ALONG "THE STREET"

VIEW FROM THE COMMON

DEERFIELD'S CIVIL WAR MONUMENT

The changes that were made in the 19th century were tasteful. In 1867 a red stone Civil War monument was erected on the common, on the site of the fourth meeting house.

Preservation was also helped when Deerfield Academy opened its doors here in 1799, after its charter was approved in 1797 by Samuel Adams, then Governor of Massachusetts.

As the institution prospered, many of the town's historic buildings were bought and restored by the school and its faculty.

DEERFIELD ACADEMY

DEERFIELD PLAYING FIELD

Old Harrow Meadow, part of the rich delta land farmed by early settlers, became a playing field, not a housing development.

Deerfield Academy is a coeducational boarding school whose motto, "Be worthy of your heritage," has guided generations of its graduates.

DEERFIELD ACADEMY'S SCENIC CAMPUS

GREENFIELD c. 1838 Courtesy J.W. Bower Historic Collection

ORIGINAL INDIAN HOUSE Author's collection

Deerfield was also lucky when, in 1811, it lost out to Greenfield in the competition to become the seat of Franklin County. What seemed like an insult at the time turned out to be a blessing in disguise.

Greenfield has its own special attractions, but where Deerfield retained its small-town charm, Greenfield became a large town with a population over four times that of Deerfield.

Deerfield also benefited from the vigorous efforts of preservationists and historians throughout most of its history. The house that resisted the Indian attack of 1704 became known as the Old Indian House and lasted until 1847, when it was dismantled.

Ensign John Sheldon had built the house in 1698. One of Ensign Sheldon's descendants, George Sheldon (1818-1916), wrote *The History of Deerfield*.

This noted antiquarian organized a remarkable collection of Deerfield artifacts in 1880 in Memorial Hall – one of Deerfield Academy's first buildings.

One of those artifacts was the original Old Indian House door – still showing the marks of the 1704 attack.

Deerfield's good fortune – and ours – continued when Mr. and Mrs. Henry N. Flynt's son enrolled at Deerfield Academy in 1936. The Flynts fell in love with the historic village and became its major benefactors. From the mid-1940s to the mid-1960s they spearheaded the acquisition and restoration of historic 18th and 19th century homes and collected furniture and precious artifacts from the area.

The Historic Deerfield houses feature authentically furnished rooms, charming oil portraits, 18th and 19th century rugs, museum-quality porcelain and silver pieces, and a comprehensive display of everyday objects from pewter measures to old fire irons.

GEORGE SHELDON
Courtesy Pocumtuck Valley Memorial Association

OLD INDIAN HOUSE DOOR

MR. AND MRS. HENRY N. FLYNT c. 1960 Courtesy Historic Deerfield

DEERFIELD *Today*

OLD BURYING GROUND OF DEERFIELD

Deerfield, then, is really three glorious attractions that reinforce one another: an historic village that has preserved much of its past, the location of one of the country's finest college preparatory schools and Historic Deerfield, incorporated in 1952, which is perhaps best described as a museum of houses.

Memories of the town's inspiring past abound. Just off The Street, the Old Burying Ground of Deerfield contains the remains of early settlers, including the forty-eight Deerfield residents slain in the 1704 attack. The gray and red slate markers bear testimony to the pioneer spirit that created and maintained this frontier outpost during the decades of the French and Indian Wars.

In 1782 the Rev. William Bentley of Salem wrote after visiting Deerfield, "The street is one measured mile [containing] about 60 houses in better style than in any Towns I saw." This broad road through the center of Deerfield is as graceful and in as good style 200 years later.

In 1929 the Old Indian House was rebuilt in the same style and form as the original and is now the Indian House Memorial Children's Museum.

THE STREET: A MEASURED MILE OF BEAUTY AND STYLE

The unparalleled collection of homes that the Flynts bought, restored and filled with their collections over fifty years ago offers an unusual opportunity to see homes from the 18th and 19th centuries, filled with authentic antiques.

INDIAN HOUSE MEMORIAL CHILDREN'S MUSEUM, OLD DEERFIELD

OLD DEERFIELD

DWIGHT-BARNARD HOUSE

THE PARSONAGE

Historic Deerfield's Museum Houses

Wright House (1824)
Parson Jonathan Ashley House (1734, 1757)
Sheldon-Hawks House (1755/1802)
Hinsdale and Anna Williams House (1816-17)
Henry N. Flynt Silver & Metalware Collection (1814 house)
Helen G. Flynt Textile Museum (1872 barn)
The Allen House (1720, 1734/1945) Flynt Residence
Rev. John Farwell Moors House (1848)
Asa Stebbins House (1799)
The Hall Tavern (built about 1765, enlarged about 1810)
Frary House (built about 1760, enlarged about 1796)
The Barnard Tavern (about 1795)
Wells-Thorn House (1746/47)
Dwight-Barnard House (built about 1725, enlarged about 1754)

Some are original homes from Old Deerfield, others were moved here. All the houses are impeccably maintained and well landscaped, with carefully trimmed lawns.

The Dwight-Barnard House (c. 1725) was dismantled in Springfield in 1950 and re-erected in Deerfield in 1954. It is now a museum displaying fine furniture, paintings, and English ceramics. The three-part color scheme is based on microscopic analysis of paint samples taken from the façade.

Jonathan Hoyt built a distinguished house in the Cheapside area of Deerfield in 1775. It was moved to its present site in 1865, where it served as the Parsonage for the First Church of Deerfield.

THE WRIGHT HOUSE

THE BARNARD TAVERN

The Wright house was built in 1824 by Asa Stebbins as a gift for his son, who was married that year. The name is taken from that of the second owner. Asa Stebbins was a forceful member of the committee that planned the Brick Church. The fence is a faithful reproduction of an earlier one.

The Barnard Tavern was built in 1795. It served as a community gathering place where one could chat with neighbors, read a newspaper or simply enjoy a drink.

Historic Deerfield maintains fourteen treasured houses as museums. Each house tour takes about 20 minutes. You need to allow 2 ½ to 3 hours for the entire walking tour.

THE FIRST CHURCH OF DEERFIELD

INTERIOR OF FIRST CHURCH

There is a rich abundance of other historic buildings in Deerfield. The Brick Church – the First Church of Deerfield – is a Federal-style meeting house that sits on the north end of the Common. The first meeting house in Deerfield was built sometime before 1675. The current church, designed by Winthrop Clapp, was built in 1824.

Services are still held regularly in this historic church.

ON THE STEPS

THE WHITE CHURCH 1838

The church steps have been the scene of many a gathering.

The other historic church in Deerfield is the Orthodox Congregational Church, known as the White Church. This was founded by Trinitarian Congregationalists opposed to the Unitarian leanings of the First Church. It is now used as a Community Center.

Deerfield is one of those towns blessed with residents who have insisted that newer town structures adhere to the architectural excellence of its historic homes. For example, the Deerfield Town Hall, erected in 1895, has now become its own classic.

FORMER TOWN HALL

MUSEUM STORE

Deerfield has created a tasteful infrastructure to help visitors enjoy its history without cluttering the town with commercial establishments that would degrade its character. A small museum store sits adjacent to the Deerfield Inn.

The Deerfield Inn (www.deerfieldinn.com), with its dazzling white columns, was built in 1884. It has welcomed generations of visiting parents and visitors with its twenty-three bedrooms (eleven in the main inn) and superb restaurant. The Inn is a convenient and charming place to stay in the center of Old Deerfield. The Deerfield Inn hosts a Strawberry Festival, Asparagus Social and Cinder Day each year in connection with the Community Involved in Sustaining Agriculture.

Deerfield has a rich array of museums and libraries. The Henry N. Flynt Silver & Metalware Collection and the Helen G. Flynt Textile Museum are part of Historic Deerfield. The Flynt Center of Early New England Life was opened in 1998 and is a decorative arts center.

Don't miss visiting the oldest museum in Deerfield, which is on Memorial Street, just beyond the White Church and former Town Hall. The sign for the Memorial Hall Museum makes it clear that this will be a special treat.

Memorial Hall Museum

A NEW ENGLAND HISTORICAL MUSEUM
POCUMTUCK VALLEY MEMORIAL ASSOCIATION

In 1870 George Sheldon organized the Pocumtuck Valley Memorial Association to collect and preserve material "which may tend to illustrate the history of by-gone generations, both Indian and English." In 1879, having come into possession of Deerfield Academy's original brick building, Memorial Hall, the association raised the top story three feet, covered the building with a tin roof and created what would become one of the oldest museums in New England.

The museum has three floors of Native American artifacts, historic clothing, ceramics, tools, an extensive collection of

MEMORIAL HALL MUSEUM

quilts, furniture, decorative arts, photographs, paintings and all manner of arts and crafts. There is a colonial kitchen, a late 19th century schoolroom and several Victorian-era rooms.

The museum has continued to acquire material that helps the visitor understand the history, culture and traditions of all the people of Western Massachusetts.

Memorial Hall Museum

8 Memorial Street
Deerfield, MA 01342
Telephone: 413-774-3768
Association website: www.old-deerfield.org

For an extensive and balanced perspective of the raid on Deerfield from the perspective of all five cultures involved, see
www.1704.deerfield.history.museum

Material is also available at
www.americancenturies.mass.edu/

In 2003 the museum purchased a traditional Iroquois ribbon dress and shawl. The artist's six-year-old daughter, Alana Teiakotewesonte Simon, is shown modeling the dress, complete with accessories.

A popular display in the museum is a painted canvas banner labeled "Mack the Giant Ox," which is shown below. Mack was the largest ox in the world in 1900. James Dean Avery (1848-1922) of Buckland raised oversized Holstein cattle as a hobby, exhibiting them at fairs and agricultural shows. The banner showing Mack and Mr. Avery hung outside Avery's display tent and now covers a good bit of the wall of the third-floor tool room.

MACK AND MR. AVERY Courtesy of the Pocumtuck Valley Memorial Association, Memorial Hall Museum, Deerfield, Massachusetts

GIRL'S RIBBON DRESS By Valerie Tewisha, photograph courtesy of the Pocumtuck Valley Memorial Association, Memorial Hall Museum, Deerfield, Massachusetts

There is plenty to do in Deerfield. The Blake Meadow Walk winds past farmland on its way to the Deerfield River. Bicycle riding is quite popular. There are horse-drawn carriage rides in summer and sleigh rides available in the winter. The town celebrates special events on Patriot's Day, Washington's Birthday and Thanksgiving. Each summer there is an Antique and Classic Car Show. An Old Deerfield Craft Fair is held in June and September.

For general information and tour reservations of Historic Deerfield call 413-774-5581. An extensive website with further information and a schedule of current events is available at www.historic-deerfield.org.

SOUTH
Deerfield

YANKEE CANDLE COMPLEX IN SOUTH DEERFIELD

Deerfield is an ideal departure point for touring the Upper Pioneer Valley.

The immediately adjacent highway (Routes 5 and 10) is a busy road sprinkled with "modern" tourist attractions, the most prominent of which is the sprawling Yankee Candle Factory complex in nearby South Deerfield (877-636-7707).

The Magic Wings Butterfly Conservatory & Gardens is open all year (413-665-2805; www.magicwings.com). The Old Deerfield Country Store (413-774-3045) is another popular family destination.

The fall is an ideal time to be in the Upper Pioneer Valley, particularly if you are small enough to perch on a pumpkin pile.

We recommend heading south on Route 5 to pick up Route 116 going east. This will take you through the center of South Deerfield. On the edge of South Deerfield there is an entrance to Mount Sugarloaf State Reservation.

PUMPKIN SITTER AT THE OLD
DEERFIELD COUNTRY STORE

The summit of Sugarloaf offers a stunning view of the Pioneer Valley and the town of Sunderland. The view is breathtaking in early October when the foliage peaks.

Before continuing on Route 116 over the Connecticut River, consider a short side trip down River Road into the eastern third of Whately.

TOWER AT TOP OF MOUNT SUGARLOAF

VIEW OF SUNDERLAND FROM MOUNT SUGARLOAF

Whately

Whately was settled about 1750 and incorporated April 24, 1771. At the end of 19th century it still had over 150 farms, with many acres of shade tobacco under cultivation. These days the area is filled with pick-your-own farms, most of them family owned. The area is famous for asparagus.

Two thirds of Whately and its historic center is on the "other" side (west) of Interstate 91, which bisects the town. In addition to the town offices, the center boasts a massive milk bottle display that celebrates the town's past as a dairy center.

Some of the best fruit and vegetable stands in New England can be found along River Road, which branches off Route 116 before the Connecticut River.

Nourse Farms, at 41 River Road, one of the largest, has a well-organized picking program that begins with strawberries in mid-June and blueberries and raspberries in mid-July.

THE QUONQUONT FARM
DISPLAY AT WHATELY CENTER

YOU PICK THEM, YOU EAT THEM

As you head back towards Route 116 there is a good view of Mount Sugarloaf. The Pocumtuck people called this formation Wequamps for a huge beaver that "many, many suns in the past" attacked the natives who lived around what was then a large lake. According to Indian legend, Hobomuck, a benevolent spirit giant, killed the beaver, who sank to the bottom of the lake and turned to stone. The Pocumtucks believed Mount Sugarloaf was the head of the beaver. You can decide for yourself.

For another view of Mount Sugarloaf and further exploration of the Pioneer Valley farmland, drive north (about two miles) on River Road. The Pine Nook Cemetery, nestled against a grove of trees, is quite picturesque.

When you return to Route 116 heading east you will cross the Connecticut River into Sunderland, the next stop on our journey.

SUGARLOAF MOUNTAIN

PINE NOOK CEMETERY

Sunderland

Sunderland is now a sizeable community of about 3,400 offering housing for students and teachers from the five-college area. The town has a long, proud history. Originally called Swampfield, the area was first settled in the 1660s but abandoned just before the start of King Philip's War in 1675. Forty families from Hadley and Hatfield petitioned for the right to resettle Swampfield in 1713 and were given permission "as long as a learned orthodox minister be settled among them." The town's historic church is part of that early legacy.

Sunderland has benefited from the community spirit and loyalty of its residents since it was incorporated in 1718. The original Graves Memorial Library now houses the aptly named Swampfield Historical Society.

John Long Graves

(1831-1915)

Thomas Graves was one of the town's first forty settlers. Horatio Graves (seventh generation) was born in Sunderland in 1788. He maintained a general store with a small one-room lending library on the second floor. His son John Long Graves became a minister, then an insurance agent, but for the last thirty-seven years of his life owned and operated an import business in Boston. He succeeded quite well in business and helped fund the town library in 1900 with an $8,200 donation. The Graves family had a strong connection to Emily Dickinson (John Long was her cousin).

JOHN LONG GRAVES
(1831-1915) Courtesy
Swampfield Historical
Society

GRAVES MEMORIAL LIBRARY
SWAMPFIELD HISTORICAL SOCIETY

SUNDERLAND FIRST CONGREGATIONAL CHURCH

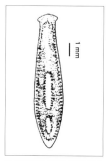

SUNDERLAND SPRING PLANARIAN Source Massachusetts Division of Fishes & Wild Life

Sunderland has a number of natural and manmade attractions. A unique freshwater flatworm – the Sunderland Spring Planarian – is found only in a cold spring in Sunderland where the water temperature is 8.5 to 9.0 degrees Celsius throughout the year. It is in the state's endangered species program.

The Sunderland Fish Hatchery along Route 116, one of only four in the state, is a quiet oasis. Massachusetts stocks dozens of ponds and streams with several species of trout (brook, rainbow, brown and lake trout).

The largest sycamore tree east of the Mississippi is in Sunderland. This is sometimes referred to as a buttonball tree.

Plenty of family farms are still in operation, such as Warner Farm, started in the 1790s. The ninth generation of Warners create an annual corn maze, cut in late August. Mike's Amazing Maze features famous figures like King Tut. Warner Farm is located on Route 47, close to the Route 116 intersection. See www.mikesmaze.com.

Sunderland's Mount Toby State Forest is popular with hikers and mountain bikers.

SUNDERLAND'S SPECTACULAR SYCAMORE

FISH HATCHERY AT SUNDERLAND

Courtesy of Warner Farm

MIKE'S KING TUT MAZE

What the *New York Times* has called "the best bar-b-que joint in New England" is in Sunderland. Bub's Bar-B-Q, founded in 1979, is now run by Bub's son and daughter-in-law. (413-548-9630; www.bubsbbq.com)

From the center of Sunderland, Route 47 south will take you to the historic town of Hadley, one of the most important communities in the colonial era.

THE BEST AND MESSIEST RIBS IN NEW ENGLAND

Hadley

1787 FARMHOUSE ALONG ROUTE 47

Route 47 is a country road with an abundance of interesting barns and old farmhouses.

Present-day Hadley occupies a long, narrow strip of land that parallels the east bank of the Connecticut River for some dozen miles.

In the early 19th century, the Pioneer Valley countryside around Hadley was considered among the most scenic in America. In 1836, Hudson River School artist Thomas Cole (1825–1870) painted "The Oxbow," featuring a scenic bend in the Connecticut River. This painting now hangs in the Metropolitan Museum of Art in New York City.

Another attraction along Route 47 is the Porter-Phelps-Huntington Museum (housed in a home built in 1752 and unchanged structurally since 1799). This complex contains the belongings of seven generations of a wealthy and productive 18th century family. It is open from May to October.

THOMAS COLE'S "THE OXBOW"

Porter-Phelps-Huntington Museum

Open: May 15 through October 15 (by appointment the rest of the year).

Guided tours: Saturday to Wednesday, 1:00 to 4:30 p.m., in season.

Folk music concerts and storytelling: June-August

130 River Drive, Hadley MA · Phone: 413-584-5699

PORTER-PHELPS-HUNTINGTON HOUSE

VIEW OF HADLEY COMMON FROM END OF WEST STREET

Hadley, which was named after a town in England, has the longest common in Massachusetts. The mile-long Hadley Common extends from Bay Road to the Connecticut River.

Norwottuck Rail Trail

From 1887-1980 the Boston and Main Railroad operated trains that went through Northampton, Hadley and Amherst. In 1985 the state purchased ten miles of the railroad right-of-way, ripped up 14,000 rail ties, and created a magnificent trail that accommodates cyclists, skaters, walkers, runners and even cross-country skiers.

Much of the trail passes through open farmland. You can enter the trail from the Hadley Common.

For more information, see www.hadleyonline.com/railtrail

HADLEY VIEW

If you get to Hadley, be sure to drive along both sides of the common (West Street) to enjoy the historic homes.

Busy Route 9 cuts right through the town (and bisects the Common). Navigation in the center of Hadley at peak hours can be frustrating, but is still well worth it. At the intersection of Route 47 (Middle Street) and Route 9 there is a handsome town hall, an historic church and the renowned Hadley Farm Museum.

FIRST CONGREGATIONAL CHURCH

HADLEY FARM MUSEUM

The museum is housed in an authentic old barn built in 1782 and moved to the present site in 1930. The exterior was remodeled to blend with the neighborhood. The barn interior is original.

Hadley Farm Museum

At the junction of Route 9 and Route 47
Open May to October
Hours: Tues. Sat. 10:00 to 4:30; Sun. 1:30 to 4:30
www.hadleyonline.com/farmmuseum

When you complete your tour of Hadley, double back on Route 47 (going north). Watch for the sign for the Riverside Cemetery, on your left, just over the Hadley – Sunderland line. This

cemetery is perfectly sited along the Connecticut River and is bathed in the light of the setting sun at dusk.

Turn right on Route 116 (heading southeast) for about two miles past the center of Sunderland, then turn left on Bull Road, which will connect you with Route 63. Take Depot Road to the center of Leverett, the next town on our journey.

RIVERSIDE CEMETERY

Leverett

Leverett is a charming town nestled in the wooded hills above the Pioneer Valley. The town's fortunate location, away from major highways, gives the community a rural feel, even though it is only seven miles from the bustling college town of Amherst.

The area was first settled in the early 1700s when it was part of Swampfield Plantation (current-day Sunderland). It was incorporated March 5, 1774, and named after John Leverett (1616-1679), a former governor of the Massachusetts Bay Colony whose grandson of the same name became president of Harvard University.

The original and still vibrant nucleus of this historic town, Leverett Center, is a two-mile-long historic district that includes the Town Hall and Congregational Church and no less than 34 historic 18th and 19th century houses, many located along Depot and Montague Roads.

LEVERETT MASSACHUSETTS HISTORICAL CENTER

Historical and Architectural Tour 2004

In 2004 the Leverett Historical Commission produced a marvellous twenty-seven-page brochure that offers a detailed tour of the historical and architectural highlights of Leverett.

Leverett Center was established in the fall of 1774 when the residents "voted by a great majority to set ye house for public worship on the hill near ye southeast corner of ye pond called fish pond." This enticing body of water, now called Leverett Pond, is about a half-milelong. It is a center of boating, fishing, and birding and contributes to the tranquil atmosphere for which Leverett is noted.

LEVERETT POND

LEVERETT FIRST CONGREGATIONAL CHURCH 1838

An orthodox house of worship was required by the General Court of Massachusetts in order to approve a petition for the establishment of a separate town. The Meeting House served as both town hall and church until 1845, when the Town Hall was built. The first Congregational Church of Leverett, an excellent example of a Greek Revival country church, was built in 1838 on the site of the original Meeting House.

As you drive along Montague Road keep an eye out for the Leverett Crafts and Arts Center. This nonprofit artist center is located in the former Beaman-Marvel Box Company. The facility includes studios where visiting artists work, plus a gift shop and gallery. Further information is available at 413-548-9070.

After touring Leverett Center, drive north on Montague Road until it intersects with Cave Hill Road, which will take you higher into the hills of Leverett. On the right you will see a sign for the Peace Pagoda, well worth a visit. The structure itself is about a half-mile hike from the parking lot, up a dirt road.

The Pagoda, a brilliant white 75-foot-high structure, appears suddenly as you round a bend.

Technically this is a stupa, which is a monument to Buddha containing a small bit of his ashes. Stupas are built with no interior rooms. Practicing Buddists will circle around the structure at the end of a pilgrimage and pray in front of the statues placed on all four sides.

The Peace Pagoda was built by young Americans led by Japanese monks and nuns of the *Nipponzan Myohoji* order of Buddhism, several of whom still reside at the complex. The order was started in the 1200s by Nichiren, a great Japanese Buddhist saint. He renewed ancient practices contained in the *Lotus Sutra*, a sacred Buddhist text. The essence of this Sutra is dedication to a world of peace.

THE PEACE PAGODA

Nichiren's school was re-energized by Nichidatsu Fuji (1885-1985), also known affectionately as Fujii Guruji, and it was his inspiration that led to the creation of close to 100 peace pagodas around the world. Nichidatsu Fuji was a friend of Mahatma Ghandi, and many of the structures were built in India, the original home of Buddhism. There are only two in the United States. (The other is in Grafton, N.Y.)

To the right of the Peace Pagoda is a Japanese Garden complete with a reflecting pool and a pavilion.

Continuing north on Cave Hill Road will take you to the heart of North Leverett. Much of Leverett's industrial activity was centered in North Leverett and a hamlet known as Moores Corner. In the last decades of the 19th century grist mills, lumber yards, a mill for carding wool, a furniture factory and a company that specialized in making wooden buckets were located here, primarily along the Sawmill River.

New England Peace Pagoda

Nipponzan Myohoji Sangha
100 Cave Hill Road
Leverett, MA 01054
413-367-2202
www.peacepagoda.org

This six-mile river, which starts at Lake Wyola in nearby Shutesbury, has a steep vertical drop (571 feet), an ideal environment for manufacturing when water power was the primary source of energy.

You will see a magnificent pond, water mill and the collapsed Watermill Lumber Company on your left. The Mill has a long 36-foot carriage for sawing lumber.

JAPANESE GARDEN AT PEACE PAGODA

The hulls for many of the minesweepers built in the early days of WWII were fabricated here.

Much of the sawmill still remains. The owners are working to restore the mill.

Continue north to the village of Moores Corner. The former one-room schoolhouse is now the headquarters of the Leverett Historical Society.

WATERMILL LUMBER COMPANY RUINS

SAWMILL RIVER DAM BEHIND MILL

BACK OF WATERMILL LUMBER CO. WITH BAPTIST CHURCH
IN BACKGROUND

The schoolhouse contains memorabilia and papers of Ruby
Hemenway (1884-1987). Born on a farm in North Leverett,
Hemenway was an important contributor to the *Dictionary of
Regional Colloquial English*. In 1976, at the age of 82, she began
writing a weekly column, "I Remember When," for the
Greenfield Recorder. Word of this remarkable woman spread.
Yankee Magazine wrote an article about the "Oldest Newspaper
Columnist on Earth." She was on Charles Kuralt's American
Parade, interviewed by National Public Radio when she was 99
years old and even invited to appear on the Johnny Carson
Show, an invitation she
declined because it would have
required a flight to California.
Ruby continued her column
until a couple years before her
death in 1987.

After exploring Moores Corner
we recommend you go down
North Leverett Road (west) to
the Routes 47 and 63
intersection (about nine miles)
to explore Montague Center.

MOORES CORNER SCHOOLHOUSE

Montague Center

The town of Montague consists of five villages, of which Montague Center is the best preserved. Montague, originally the north parish of Sunderland, was settled between 1715 and 1730 and incorporated in 1753. It was named for Captain William Montague, a prominent soldier during the long conflict between England and France.

Montague Center is a charming crossroads village organized around a well-preserved green. The common is ringed by churches and a sturdy brick town hall built in 1858, when this was the governing center of Montague. The village is noted for its many 19th century Greek Revival style homes and a large amount of undeveloped land. Located along the Sawmill River, Montague Center became a hub of commercial activities in an era when grist mills, sawmills and light manufacturing predominated.

MILLS ALONG THE SAWMILL RIVER IN MONTAGUE c. 1880

MONTAGUE COMMON

By the end of the 19th century the center of manufacturing had shifted to the Montague village of Turners Falls and to nearby Greenfield. Montague Center gradually returned to its rural roots.

A millstone from a colonial grist mill of 1725 sits on the common. It is located at the site of the village's first schoolhouse.

Montague Center still has plenty of productive farmland and retains an open, pastoral feel. There is a 1,425-acre Wildlife Management area just minutes from the common where one can walk, watch birds and picnic in the town's splendid meadows. The back country roads in the hills – many dating to the 18th century – are favorite destinations for biking.

The First Congregational Church of Montague, built in 1834, anchors one end of the common. Every August the town holds an event-filled, two-day Old Home Days festival, sponsored by the Congregational Church.

BICYCLING IN THE BUCOLIC COUNTRYSIDE
OF MONTAGUE CENTER

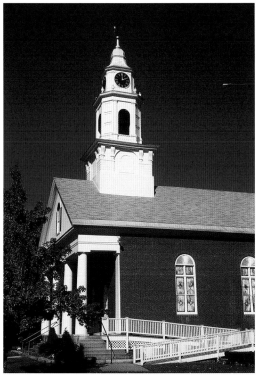

FIRST CONGREGATIONAL CHURCH OF MONTAGUE

The Montague Grange, on the Common, is a center of art and craft shows and community events.

On May 1 there is a day-long festival heralding the arrival of spring with traditional maypole dancing, group singing and performances.

THE MONTAGUE GRANGE

HARTSBROOK GARLAND TEAM DANCING AT
MAY 1 CELEBRATION Courtesy Montague Historical Society

CARRYING THE MAY POLE, MAY DAY 2005
Courtesy Montague Historical Society

JACKIE ROBINSON USED A LOUISVILLE SLUGGER

THE BOOK MILL

One mill remains from the early days. The former Alvah Sone Grist Mill became home to the Martin Machine Shop, which manufactured the metal stamp that burned "Louisville Slugger" into millions of baseball bats.

Today this old mill now houses artist studios and a rambling bookstore (appropriately called the Book Mill). The complex is less than a mile north of the Grange Hall.

The Book Mill has an eclectic mixture of new and used books. Owner David Lovelace once described its role as "selling books you don't need in a place you can't find." This might have been the case once, but the Book Mill is now a focal point of community activity and a "must" destination for tourists in the know.

A GREAT PLACE FOR BOOKS
(INTERIOR OF THE BOOK MILL)

There are several craft shops in the total complex and spots outside and inside where you can relax and catch a bite to eat.

A deck in back of the Montague Mill offers a pleasant spot to sit and be mesmerized by swirling currents in the Sawmill River as they flow by.

When you can tear yourself away, make your way to Route 63.

RELAX AND REFRESH
ON THE DECK

SAWMILL RIVER FLOWING BEHIND THE BOOK MILL

LAKE

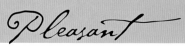

Pleasant

LAKE PLEASANT COTTAGE c. 1890
Courtesy of Montague Historical
Society

JOYCE COTE AT THE POST OFFICE

A few miles beyond Montague Center, just off Route 63, is the village of Lake Pleasant, another of the five villages of Montague. George Potter of nearby Greenfield developed picnic grounds here in 1870.

In 1876, however, the New England Spiritualist Association acquired the Lake Pleasant property. The Spiritualist connection lured thousands each summer to enjoy the waters, listen to musical entertainment, and attend lectures and séances. Families began spending the summers here, and rustic cabins soon replaced the original tents.

A devastating fire in 1907 burned much of the village, and the advent of the automobile created more interesting vacation opportunities. Then, in the 1920s the magician Houdini exposed the séance "experiences" as elaborate tricks, which he reproduced. But the glory days of Lake Pleasant were already largely over.

The U.S Post Office, ably run by Joyce Cote, is now the major community center.

The National Spiritual Alliance, which evolved from the New England Spiritualist Association that once owned Lake Pleasant, still operates a "temple" across from the Post Office, where it gives courses on handwriting analysis, stages psychic fairs and

BRIDGE OF NAMES

holds a Sunday afternoon service that includes hands-on healing.

If you do get to Lake Pleasant, be sure to stroll across its bridge. A deep gorge divides Lake Pleasant into two communities, and there has been a footbridge connecting them for years.

NAMES ON THE BRIDGE

The current bridge was built in 1976 with donations from current and former residents and their descendants, who are each acknowledged on the wooden slats that line the sides of the walkway.

This "Bridge of Names" and the splendid lake (now a reservoir for the town of Montague) have become minor tourist attractions.

The Pioneer Valley continues beyond Montague and its villages, but the principal towns of Greenfield and Northfield are best seen as part of a journey along Route 2 (see the Pathways to the Past Guide: *Along the Mohawk Trail*).

ON TO CONWAY

Significant additional attractions await us southwest of Deerfield, easily reached by returning to Route 116 again, this time going west, toward Conway. Take Route 47 south for about five miles to reach Route 116 (see map).

The Massachusetts maple sugar industry is concentrated (pun intended) in Western Massachusetts.

Boyden Bros. Sugarhouse, on the outskirts of Conway, is one of about a dozen primary maple sugar producers in Franklin County.

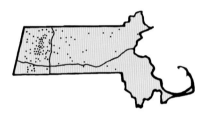

MAPLE SUGAR PRODUCERS AND SUGARHOUSES

INTERESTING MAPLE SYRUP FACTS

· There are thirteen native maple tree species in North America, but the two most commonly tapped are sugar maple (Acer Saccharum) and black maple (Acer Nigrum).

· Pure maple syrup is made by concentrating the slightly sweet sap of the sugar maple tree.

· A maple tree must be a least 10 inches in diameter and in good health before it can be tapped. It usually takes about forty years before a tree will reach tappable size.

· Throughout the 4-6 week sugar season, each tap hole will yield about ten gallons of sap. This is only a small portion of the tree's total sap production and will not hurt the tree. The average amount of syrup that can be made from ten gallons of sap is about one quart.

BOYDEN BROS. SUGARHOUSE

- A healthy sugar maple can provide sap every year for 100 years or more.

- Maple syrup is traditionally made in a building called a "sugarhouse," named for the time when most sap was actually turned into sugar.

- Sugarhouses vary from rustic wood buildings with no electricity hidden out in the woods to modern food-processing plants.

- All sugarhouses have a vent (cupola) at the top to allow the steam of the boiling syrup to escape. Steam rising from the cupola is a sign that maple syrup season is under way.

MAPLE INFORMATION: The Massachusetts Maple phone number is 413-628-3912. From late February through early April, a recording about the boiling season is updated.

Conway

CONWAY HISTORICAL SOCIETY QUILT

TREASURES LIE JUST OFF THE ORDINARY-
LOOKING HIGHWAY

The town of Conway wasn't settled until the end of the French
and Indian Wars and was eventually incorporated in 1767.

Conway has a rich tradition and an active Historical Society.
The Historical Society quilt (made by early members of the
group) is in great demand at exhibitions.

You might be tempted to pass through Conway, whose center
straddles Route 116 and is not particularly picturesque, but you
would be making a mistake.

Pull over to the side of the road, and look back. Nestled in the
foothills at the edge of town is a magnificent Greek Revival
building which houses the Field Library...upon which turns a tale.

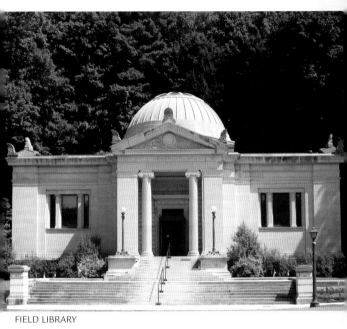

FIELD LIBRARY

ENTRANCE TO FIELD LIBRARY

The library was donated to the town in 1901 by its most famous son, the merchant Marshall Field. Field personally selected the site and hired a Boston architect to design the structure named to honor his parents.

PRODUCED IN CONWAY

NOT JUST TISSUE, "SILK" TISSUE

For a number of years Archibald MacLeish, the poet and another famous Conway resident, served as one of the trustees.

Conway has a fascinating history. It was originally a farming community, but farming began to decline in the 1860s as its young people headed west. So Conway transformed itself into a major manufacturing center.

There have been over fifty mills and factories in Conway over the years, starting with a grist mill in 1767.

A visit to the Conway Historical Society is a step back into a time when Massachusetts was a manufacturing powerhouse. By the 1800s Conway housed over a dozen sawmills, tanneries, brickyards, and all manner of small-scale manufacturing.

Marshall Field

(1835-1906)

Marshall Field was born in Conway. He spent his boyhood on a farm and attended local schools until he was seventeen. He started out as a dry goods clerk in Pittsfield, Massachusetts, then moved to Chicago and became a junior partner in the merchant house that became Field, Palmer & Leiter. By 1881

he was the head and almost sole owner of Marshall Field & Company, which was destined to become one of the largest wholesale and retail dry goods businesses in the world. Field was the source and inspiration of the ideas that revolutionized retail selling everywhere. He never forgot his roots in Conway and named several of his products after the town.

UNITED CONGREGATIONAL CHURCH

Perhaps the most famous Conway product was the "silk tissue" marketed by its native son, Marshall Field. (Oh for an era where you went to a department store to buy toilet paper.)

Conway consisted of a dozen or so villages that were the real heart of the town. Go back a hundred yards or so on Route 116 east, just beyond the Field Library and Town Hall, and take the Whately–Conway road. This leads to Pumpkin Hollow, one of Conway's most picturesque neighborhoods. The United Congregational Church you will pass is still serving the community.

STONE WALL WITH PUMPKIN ON DISPLAY

BURKEVILLE COVERED BRIDGE IN PROCESS OF RESTORATION

The roads to the south of Route 116 take you back into rural areas, country roads lined with stone fences – and an occasional pumpkin displayed in the fall.

CONWAY BURKEVILLE BRIDGE FROM CHURCH IN FALL

After returning to Route 116, heading west out of town, keep an eye out for the Burkeville Covered Bridge on the left. For most of the last few years this bridge has been closed and obscured by scrubs and vines, but the renovation of this gem finally started in 2004, and it will soon be a major attraction.

The bridge was originally built in 1869. When it is reopened as a footbridge you will be able to appreciate how well it is sited – now apparent only in the fall.

Just across from the Burkeville Bridge, on a knoll overlooking Route 116, is St. Mark's Catholic Church. It was built in 1869 to serve the new mix of Irish and other European immigrants that arrived in Conway to work in the local factories.

ENTRANCE TO ST. MARK'S CHURCH

Those who are fascinated by old bridges will want to make their way through North Conway to the Bardwell Ferry Bridge.

This is one of the oldest and longest single-span lenticular truss bridges in New England, fully 198 feet in length.

It was built by the Berlin Iron Bridge Company in 1882. In 1988 this bridge was designated a Historic Civil Engineering Landmark.

BARDWELL FERRY BRIDGE
Photo courtesy of Dr. Alan Lutenegger

About 100 lenticular truss bridges were built in the Commonwealth of Massachusetts between 1878 and 1895. According to Professor Alan Lutenegger of the University of Massachusetts, only nine are known to still exist.

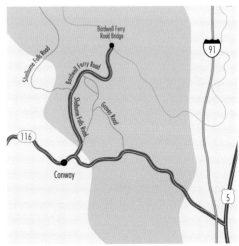

MAP TO BARDWELL FERRY BRIDGE

Ashfield

ASHFIELD EPISCOPAL CHURCH 1828

As you head west again on Route 116, the land continues to rise gently. These are the eastern foothills of the Green Mountains.

The next town is Ashfield, which was initially named Huntstown in honor of Captain Ephraim Hunt. Captain Hunt played a key role in one of the many English–French conflicts known as King William's War. The descendants of Hunt's soldiers settled the town about 1745, and it was formally incorporated in 1765.

THE CHURCH IS A GATHERING
PLACE FOR THE COMMUNITY

SITE OF ZACHARIAH FIELD TAVERN 1792

Ashfield is a town blessed with great architecture. St. John's
Episcopal Church was built in 1828. Just across Main Street is
the First Congregational Church, first organized in 1763. The
present building was constructed in 1856. The entire main
street of Ashfield is a National Historic District.

The unspoiled towns along Route 116 are still small
communities where area residents worship and gather every
Sunday.

Some of Ashfield's historic structures, like the Zachariah Field
Tavern, are now residences.

NEWER BULDINGS FIT THE TOWN AMBIENCE

THE ASHFIELD HISTORICAL SOCIETY

The town's newer buildings house local businesses like the Ashfield Hardware & Supply.

In season there is a farmer's market held near the Historical Society Museum. The Ashfield Historical Society has ten rooms full of town memorabilia and a recreated general store (www.ashfieldmuseum.org).

OXEN CARRYING CORN FODDER c. 1890 by Howes Brothers

The Society is also the custodian of the priceless photographic legacy of the Howes brothers.

Alvah, Walter and George Howes traveled hundreds of miles throughout the Connecticut Valley between 1882 and 1907, documenting everyday life. Twenty-three thousand original Howes Brothers glass-plate negatives are currently being catalogued and microfilmed by the Historical Society, with local and national support.

COOPERS WITH THEIR BARRELS
By Howes Brothers

DISCERNING FARMERS MARKET SHOPPERS
MAKE A PICNIC OF THEIR PURCHASES

THERE ARE OFTEN RURAL GUIDED
TOURS—IF YOU'RE A DUCK

The weekly Ashfield farmers market features authentic local produce. You can stock up for the week or sit down with a friend to enjoy your purchase, right on the spot.

The Ashfield Town Hall was originally the town's Congregational meeting house, built in 1812. It was moved to its present location on Main Street in 1856. The steeple is an architectural gem, an octagonal shape with balustrades, surrounded by rope molding.

Outside Ashfield, the country becomes more rural; ducks swim in the streams and sunflower fields color the countryside along Route 116. Bear Swamp (a Trustees of Reservations Property on Hawley Road, about 1.7 miles from the junction of Routes 112 and 116) is a 171-acre forest preserve with three miles of trails. It feels like an untouched wilderness and is known for its wildflowers. See www.thetrustees.org.

< ASHFIELD TOWN HALL

Plainfield

SUNFLOWERS IN SUMMER

Plainfield, originally part of Cummington, was established in 1782. The original settlers came from Bridgewater and Abington (towns south of Boston). Plainfield was incorporated in 1807.

Located on the eastern edge of the Green Mountains, Plainfield is a lovely, unspoiled part of Western Massachusetts. Around a bend in the road you will invariably find a field of sunflowers … or a picturesque old farmhouse.

There are still serious working farms in Plainfield and the surrounding communities. Massachusetts farms like the Waryjasz family complex still produce almost 70 million pounds of potatoes a year. The emphasis now is on colorful red, blue and yellow potatoes as well as fingerling-shaped potatoes.

Visitors are welcome to Waryjasz (166 E. Main Street) and other Plainfield farms.

A PLAINFIELD FARMHOUSE

THE WARYJASZ FARM IS WORTH A STOP

VISIT THE WARYJASZ FARM TO SEE FARMING IN ACTION

PLAINFIELD COMMON c. 1890

PLAINFIELD COMMON TODAY

The center of Plainfield looks much as it did a century ago, with the Town Hall and Congregational Church sitting on a bluff overlooking Route 116.

The Congregational Church was first gathered in 1786.

There are picturesque sugarhouses along Route 116 and the back roads to the north and south. The Massachusetts Maple Producers Association is headquartered on Watson-Spruce Corner Road in Ashfield.

Route 116 continues in a northwesterly direction outside of Plainfield until it joins with Route 8A near the Plainfield–Hawley line.

This area is heavily forested and contains several pristine ponds.

The Dubuque State Memorial Forest offers excellent hiking.

MAPLE SUGARHOUSE OUTSIDE PLAINFIELD

BE PREPARED TO PAUSE AND ADMIRE NATURE'S WONDERS

Cummington

Photograph by Michael Tougias

WEST CUMMINGTON EPISCOPAL CHURCH

Route 8A further north is less interesting than the towns south of Route 116, so we suggest you double back and return to Plainfield.

After reaching the center of town again, turn right (south) on a well-marked rural road (South Central Street) that leads to the town of Cummington.

This is a great area for wandering the back roads.

SOUTH FACE FARM

1790 MILLSTONE AT KINGMAN TAVERN

The Lower Plainfield - South Ashfield - Cummington area has some magnificent farms. One of the gems is South Face Farm, a major maple syrup producer. The Cummington Fair (www.cummingtonfair.com), which dates to 1883, is held over four days in late August.

Cummington has two renowned attractions, beyond the charming town itself. In the center of Cummington, the Kingman Tavern Historical Museum (41 Main Street) is a four-building complex that includes a seventeen-room early 1800s house (once a tavern), a barn, a carriage shed, and an 1840s cider mill.

MAGNIFICENT MAPLES LINE THE ROAD LEADING TO
THE BRYANT HOME

WILLIAM CULLEN BRYANT HOMESTEAD

A VIEW FROM THE
BRYANT PORCH

The William Cullen Bryant Homestead is
located on Bryant Road outside
Cummington, about 1.5 miles south of
the intersection of Routes 9 and 12. A
charming road lined with maple trees
planted by Bryant and his brother leads
to the house.

This was the boyhood home and, later,
summer residence of William Cullen
Bryant, the poet and journalist. Bryant's
widowed mother was forced to sell the
home in 1835. Thirty years later he
bought it back.

Bryant, who was editor of the *New York Evening Post*, returned to this retreat often. His favorite spot was the porch. The twenty-three-room house has a commanding view of the Westfield River Valley and Hampshire Hills.

The Trustees of Reservations

- Founded in 1891, the Trustees of Reservations is dedicated to preserving properties of exceptional scenic, historic and ecological value throughout the Commonwealth of Massachusetts.
- The William Cullen Bryant Homestead, one of the eighty-three properties of the Trustees, is a National Historic Landmark. The group publishes The William Cullen Bryant Homestead Self-Guided Landscape Tour Brochure.
- Nineteen of the organization's properties are in western Massachusetts.
- The Trustees of Reservations is a nonprofit conservation organization and relies for support entirely upon membership dues, admission fees, and voluntary contributions. www.thetrustees.org/

Stop at the Old Creamery Grocery on Route 9, near the Bryant Homestead, for a snack or to enjoy the local color before heading south on Route 9 towards Goshen.

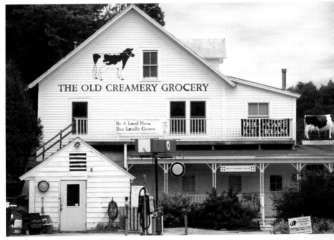

OLD CREAMERY GROCERY

Goshen

The town of Goshen, originally part of Chesterfield, was incorporated on May 14, 1781. The founders chose the name Goshen because they thought it was the "best part" of Chesterfield, just as the biblical town of Goshen was the "best part" of ancient Egypt (Genesis 45: 10,11).

The oldest house in Goshen was built in 1770 by Christopher Banister, one of five brothers who emigrated here from Brookfield. Banister served in the French and Indian Wars and attained the rank of Major in the Revolutionary War. The simple Banister Cape Cod is now headquarters for the Hampshire Riding Club.

BANISTER HOUSE 1770

The Goshen Cemetery was in use before the town was incorporated. The oldest readable headstone dates to 1774. The Cemetery is a favorite subject of artists.

THE GOSHEN CEMETERY
Courtesy Elise Engler, 1979

The town is located on hilly terrain high in the Berkshire foothills where rainfall is abundant, and the temperature is pleasant in the summer months. Early in the 20th century this rural community began to attract summer visitors to guest houses and, later, cabins erected along its abundant lakes. Goshen became host to many youth camps, a large YMCA complex and a Civilian Conservation Corps facility. When the town of Dana was flooded c. 1929 to create the Quabbin Reservoir, Camp Howe of Dana was relocated to Goshen.

The most famous summer destination in Goshen was Mountain Rest, a vacation retreat for Protestant missionaries from all over the world. Mountain Rest was created in 1902 by Dr. George D. Dowkontt of New York City, who also founded the International Medical Missionary Society.

For over six decades each summer hundreds of missionaries and their families made their way to Goshen to enjoy the healthy climate and enchanting woodlands of the town (for $5.00 a day in the early years). This cosmopolitan crowd, which ultimately hailed from over sixty countries, made Goshen a place known around the world.

A BUILDING IN THE FORMER MOUNTAIN REST COMPLEX

GOSHEN SLATE

Mountain Rest closed in 1972. The buildings are now privately held. The main house has been converted into condominiums.

Another phenomenon that put Goshen "on the map" is the town's extensive deposits of mica schist (slate).

Slate has been quarried in Goshen since the 19th century and is used all over New England for walks, terraces, walls and

GOSHEN QUARRY

facing.

There are still two active quarries in the town.

Goshen still retains many descendants of early town settlers.
The Barrus Farm has been in the family for over 200 years. Levi
Barrus first came to Goshen in 1812. One of his descendants,
Hiram Barrus, wrote the first history of Goshen, in 1881.

The Barrus Farm now has a large herd of llamas whose wool is

LLAMAS AT BARRUS FARM

lighter and warmer than sheep's wool.

Goshen is heavily wooded. The Massachusetts Chapter of the Daughters of the American Revolution donated 1,120 pristine Goshen acres to the state in 1929, to be used as a wildlife sanctuary. In subsequent years the DAR Forest was expanded to include Upper Highland Lake, where there is an inviting trail along the shoreline. On a clear day you can see five states from the Fire Tower erected on Moore's Hill in the DAR Forest, the highest point in Goshen.

Goshen's abundant streams and brooks, and ample forests, attracted sawmills in the early 19th century. By the 1830s Goshen mills, in addition to producing lumber, made broom handles, wooden pegs, wagon wheels, shingles and planes. The

RUINS OF MILL ALONG SWIFT RIVER

picturesque ruins of one of the early mills can be found along the West Branch of the Swift River, off Spruce Corner Road.

The extensive stone walls of the mill, which made wagon wheels, are still visible. Workmen from the mill were provided rooms in a large house built on high ground above the facility. This is now a private residence. The complex is known to locals as "The Land of Goshen."

Another "insider attraction" in Goshen is Lily Pond, a large bog where sphagnum moss, wild cranberries and blueberries flourish. It is a floating bog, seemingly without a bottom, which has fostered one of the best Goshen legends, that of "the stagecoach that disappeared."

"LAND OF GOSHEN"

In the mid 1800s a stagecoach line connected Goshen with Cummington and Williamsburg. The stage road forded the bog at its narrowest point with a crude bridge of logs covered with dirt and rocks. Old-timers claimed that a stagecoach veered off the road into bog late one evening and was never seen again.

LILY POND TODAY

Goshen has a well-organized Museum located in the former chapel of the Second Advent Society. The Adventists used the church from 1878 to the mid-1950s, then rented it for a few years to a Pentecostal sect. It was deeded to the Goshen Historical Society in 1973.

The original church organ is one of the prized objects in the museum.

GOSHEN MUSEUM, LOCATED ON ROUTE 9

SECOND ADVENT SOCIETY ORGAN

The Goshen Museum has a special "Artists Corner" where some of the numerous paintings depicting the town done by many generations of artists now hang.

In addition to the typical collection of farm implements, family Bibles and scrapbooks, the museum has some unusual objects.

Notable among these is a violin hand-crafted by Albert Emerson Willcutt (1860-1938), a Goshen resident who sold his violins all over New England.

The Goshen Museum is open Sundays from 2:00 to 4:00 pm from Memorial Day through Labor Day. It is located right along Route 9.

ARTISTS CORNER IN MUSEUM

As you wander in Goshen be sure to visit the Tin Man of Goshen, right along Route 112. The Tin Man (who started out life working for a local heating oil delivery company) now stands outside the Good Time Stove Company, welcoming one and all.

TIN MAN OF GOSHEN

When you are done exploring Goshen, return to Route 9 heading further east, to the final destination in our tour of the Upper Pioneer Valley, Williamsburg.

Williamsburg

The land along Route 9 becomes increasingly populated as you drive southeast into Williamsburg, which was incorporated in 1775. The town is now an important bedroom community for the college towns of nearby Northampton and Amherst.

Williamsburg has preserved its charm, though, as tasteful new buildings mix with its historic churches and the town hall.

Williamsburg was the scene of one of New England's worst disasters, when the dam on the East Branch of the Mill River collapsed on May 16, 1874, drowning 145 residents of Mill Valley. More would have been killed if the gatekeeper, a Civil War veteran named George Cheney, hadn't sounded the alarm after a frantic ride that caused him to be called "the Paul Revere of Western Massachusetts."

NEW BUILDINGS BLEND IN WITH THE OLD IN WILLIAMSBURG

WILLIAMSBURG CONGREGATIONAL CHURCH

HAYDENVILLE CHURCH

As we end this journey we encourage you to be sure to drive a few miles further south on Route 9 to the village of Haydenville, which has a splendid old church and common. The Brass Works, a converted factory complex, is also located in Haydenville.

Things to Consider

TAPPING THE MAPLE TREES

If you are seeking the best time to wander the back country roads of the Pioneer Valley, the spring and early summer months are hard to beat. June and July are optimum for picking your own berries. The fall has its own unique attractions, of course. The foliage usually peaks during the first two weeks in October.

However, this is an area that has a special charm in the winter. Cross-country skiing is quite popular, the historic houses in Deerfield are less crowded, and early March brings another maple sugar harvest.

To take advantage of the diverse attractions the Upper Pioneer Valley has to offer, finding the right place to stay and preparing for your trip are important. The final sections of this guide provide information on accommodations, key addresses and phone numbers, and sources for maps, books and websites that can help.

One thing you will find about the Upper Pioneer Valley is that subsequent visits will lead to new discoveries as the seasons change and as you venture off on different back roads. Who knows, some day you might even discover TRUTH, as we did wandering off Route 116 one summer day.

WINTER WONDERLAND

AND THAT'S THE TRUTH

Accommodations

The Upper Pioneer Valley is an ideal vacation or long weekend destination, but the quality of the total experience will depend on where you stay.

There are ample lodgings in all price brackets in the college towns of Amherst and South Deerfield and in Greenfield, the seat of Franklin County. Two established non-chain facilities are the 48-room Lord Jeffery Inn in Amherst (413-253-2576; www.lordjefferyinn.com) or The Brandt House in Greenfield (413-774-3329 – 9 guest rooms; www.brandthouse.com). For the budget minded there is a large Red Roof Inn in South Deerfield (413-665-7161).

For a special experience in the heart of the Upper Pioneer Valley we recommend several small inns and B & Bs.

Deerfield Inn is a classic country inn, built in 1884, and located in the historic town of Deerfield, featured at the beginning of our journey. The Inn has a well-regarded restaurant with menus rooted in period, regional New England cuisine.

81 Old Main Street, Deerfield, MA 01342
413-774-5587, or 1-800-926-3865
www.deerfieldinn.com
23 rooms, full service

Twin Maples, a 200-year-old colonial farmhouse located on 27 acres, about two miles from the center of Williamsburg. There is a sugarhouse on the property (in operation February-April).

106 South Street, Williamsburg, MA 01096
413-268-7925 www.twinmaplesbnb.com
3 bedrooms, shared bath

Flower Hill Farm B&B, a 20-acre hillside flower farm operated by renowned plantswoman Carol Duke, offers two suites in a 1790 restored Cape Cod style farmhouse.

Williamsburg, MA 01096
413-268-7481
www.caroldukeflowers.com
3 guest suites, a studio, 4 private baths

The Ashley Graves House, a restored 1830 farmhouse in historic Sunderland, furnished with period antiques.

121 N. Main St. (Route 47) just north of town center, Sunderland, MA 01375
413-665-6656
ashleygraveshouse.com
4 guest rooms with private baths

Clark Tavern Inn Bed & Breakfast, an authentic Revolutionary War era Georgian colonial inn moved to this location in Hadley and carefully restored.

98 Bay Rd. (just off Route 47, south of Route. 9), Hadley, MA 01035
413-586-1900 www.clarktaverninn.com
3 rooms with private baths

The Five College Area Bed and Breakfast Association maintains data on about 35 different B&B facilities, if you need additional options. See www.bbonline.com/ma/fivecollege/index.html.

The Visitors Center in Greenfield publishes a lodging guide twice a year.

Supplemental Reading

The Berkshire Hills & Pioneer Valley of Western Massachusetts, by Christina Tree & William Davis Woodstock, Vermont: Countryman Press, 2004.

Quiet Places of Massachusetts, by Michael J. Tougias, Edison, NJ: Hunter Publishing, 1996.

History of Western Massachusetts (2 Volumes) by Josiah Gilbert Holland, Springfield MA: Samuel Bowles & Co. 1855. *An early definitive study.*

New England Outpost: War and Society in Colonial Deerfield, by Richard I. Melvoin, New York, NY: W.W. Norton & Company, 1989. *A useful summary of important events.*

The Northern Colonial Frontier, 1607-1763, by Douglas E. Leach, New York: Holt, Rinehart and Winston, 1955. *Puts the Massachusetts frontier in a broader context.*

Town Planning in Frontier America, by John W. Reps, Princeton: Princeton University Press, 1969. *Origins, principles and practices.*

Early Settlement in the Connecticut Valley, by Peter Thomas, Stephen Innes and Richard I. Melvoin, Deerfield, MA: Institute for Massachusetts Studies, 1984. *A thorough accounting of the area's history.*

Conway 1767-1967, edited by Deane Lee, Conway, MA:, 1967. *Town history.*

Greenfield Gazette Centennial Edition, published February 1, 1892, on the one hundredth anniversary of the newspaper. *Discusses and illustrates each town and provides the essential history.*

The French and Indian War 1754-1763, by Seymour I. Schwartz, New York: Simon & Schuster, 1994. *A scholarly history of the conflict.*

Historic Deerfield: Houses and Interiors, by Samuel Chamberlain and Henry N. Flynt, New York, NY: Hastings House, 1972. *A comprehensive early documentation of Historic Deerfield houses and their contents.*

Montague, by Peter S. Miller and Kyle J. Scott, Charleston, SC: Arcadia Publishing, 2000. *Town history, extensively illustrated.*

Sermons in Stone: The Stone Walls of New England and New York, by Susan Allport. New York: Norton, 1990. *A fascinating discussion* *of the types and uses of stone walls and related cultural structures.*

A Long Deep Furrow: Three Centuries of Farming in New England,
by Harold S. Russell. Hanover, NH: University Press of New
England, 1976. *A well-researched explanation of the changes in New
England's agriculture.*

USEFUL CONTACTS

The Memorial Hall Museum has extensive information
available online, including the story of the raid on Deerfield
and the history of the area's Native Americans:
www.memorialhall.mass.edu/home.html

Massachusetts Office of Travel and Tourism has lots of
information and a guide at www.massvacation.com
(1-800-227-6277).

The Visitors Center at I-91 Rotary & Route 2A on Miner Street
in Greenfield (413-773-9393) offers free brochures and
information. The complex sells maps, books and memorabilia.

Massachusetts Country Roads (www.masscountryroads.com)
provides information on local weather, lodging, dining and
things to do in Western Massachusetts.

The Great Falls Discover Center in Turners Falls has extensive
displays and information on the Connecticut River;
413-863-3221.

State Parks brief descriptions and summary information on
hiking, camping and fishing at
www.masslive.com/outdoors/parks1.html.

The Massachusetts Division of Fisheries and Wildlife at
www.mass.gov/masswildlife.org (899-275-3474).

The Rubel Bicycle Maps for Western Massachusetts and
Central Massachusetts, www.bikemaps.com/index.htm#top.

Where to Bird at
www.birding.com/wheretobird/Massachusetts.asp.

The Snowmobiling Association of Massachusetts:
413-369-8092; www.sledmass.com.

Massachusetts Maple Producers Association:
www.massmaple.org. Massachusetts Maple Seasonal
hotline: 413-628-3912.

Pick-your-own sources at www.buylocalfood.com.

A handy laminated pocket guide, **Massacusetts Birds:
An Introduction to Familiar Species,** by James
Kavanagh, illustrated by Raymond Leung, Waterford
Press.

Photography Credits

Jim McElholm

Cover Images

Aerial View of Sunderland (front cover), sugarhouse, children on pumpkins and Historic Deerfield House (back cover), Ashfield Town Hall and South Face Farm (inside flap)

Book Images, listed by page

Historic Deerfield House 4
Connecticut River 8-9
Deerfield Academy Buildings ..15
Deerfield Academy Students ..15
Old Deerfield View 20
Dwight-Barnard House 20
The Parsonage 20
Wright House 21
Barnard Tavern 22
First Church of Deerfield 23
On steps of First Church 24
Deerfield Museum Store 25
Yankee Candle Complex 30
Pumpkin Sitter 31
Sunderland from
Mount Sugarloaf 32-33
Kids Carrying Strawberries 35
Child Eating Strawberries 35
1775 Grist Millstone 58
First Congregational Church ..59
Eating on Deck 63
View of Back of Montague Mill ..
63
Steps of Field Library 69
Ashfield Episcopal Church 76
Ashfield Town Hall 80
Sugarhouse Outside Plainfield 85
South Face Farm 87
Road to Bryant Housestead 88

Williamsburg General Store 98
Congregational Church 98
Tapping the Maple Trees 100
Winter Scene – Pioneer Valley 101

David J. McLaughlin

Cover Images

Waterfall – North Leverett (front cover), Watermill Lumber Company (back inside flap)

Book Images, listed by page

Old Deerfield Sign 12
A View Along "The Street" 13
Deerfield Common 13
Civil War Monument 14
Deerfield Academy Field..........15
Indian House Door 17
Deerfield Burying Ground 18
"The Street" 19
Old Indian House Today 19
Interior of First Church 23
White Church 24
1895 Town Hall......................25
Memorial Hall Museum Sign ..26
Memorial Hall Museum 27
Top of Mount Sugarloaf 31
Whately Giant Milk Bottle 34
Sugarloaf Mountain 36
Pine Nook Cemetery 37
Graves Memorial Library 38
Sunderland Church 39
Sunderland Fish Hatchery 41
Bub's Bar-B-Que 41
1787 Farmhouse 42
Cole Painting of Oxbow Turn ..43
Porter-Phelps-Huntington 43
Bicycle Path 44

Hadley Common 44
First Congregational Church,
Hadley 45
View of Hadley Fields in Spring 45
Hadley Farm Museum 46
Riverside Cemetery...................46
Leverett Booklet.......................47
Leverett Pond 48-49
First Congregational Church....50
Peace Pagoda 51
Japanese Garden 52-53
Watermill Lumber Co. 54
Sawmill River Dam..................54
Back of Watermill Lumber Co. 55
Moores Corner Schoolhouse ..55
Montague Common 56-57
Old Home Days Sign 59
Montague Grange 60
Book Mill 62
Book Mill Interior 63
Lake Pleasant Postmaster........64
Bridge of Names 65
Name Slat 65
Boydon Bros. Sugarhouse 67
Conway Quilt 68
Center of Conway 68
Field Library Set Against Hills 69
Washing Machine Museum 70
Conway Silk Tissue 70
United Congregational Church 71
Stone Fence with Pumpkin 72
Burkeville Covered Bridge........72
Covered Bridge in Fall 73
St. Mark's Church Door 74
After Church - Ashfield 77
Zachariah Field Tavern 77
Ashfield Hardware & Supply....78
Historical Society Building 78
Girls Eating Raspberries 81
Ducks Touring 81
Sunflowers 82
Farmhouse Along Route 116 ..83
Waryjasz Farm Truck 83
Waryjasz Farm Entrance..........83
Plainfield Common Today 84
Dubuque Memorial Forest 85
1790 Millstone 87

Bryant Homestead 88
Porch of Bryant House 88
Old Creamery Grocery 89
Banister House 90
Mountain Rest Building 92
Goshen Slate 92
Goshen Quarry 93
Llamas at Barrus Farm 93
Ruins of mill 94
"Land of Goshen" 95
Lily Pond 95
Goshen Museum 96
Organ 96
Violin in Goshen Museum 97
Artists Corner 97
Tin Man of Goshen 97
Haydenville Church 99
Truth Sign 101

Michael Tougias

Sunderland Sycamore Tree 40
West Cummington Church......86

Acknowledgments

I am indebted to professional photographer Jim McElholm of Single Source Inc. (508-987-0809) in Oxford, Massachusetts, for the right to use his superb photographs. The travel writer Michael Tougias provided general recommendations and made two of his images available for use in this book.

After the success of our first collaboration, it was an easy decision to partner again with Laren Bright in creating this book. His love of writing, his superb judgment and his zest for travel shaped the book in many special ways. This award-winning writer lives in the Los Angeles area and can be reached at 323-852-0433.

Cindy Wilson and her talented team designed the cover for *Exploring the Upper Pioneer Valley* and did the interior design and layout of the book. Cindy, who lives in Saint Augustine, Florida, can be reached at 904-826-1672.

Many knowledgeable individuals helped us in our research. The staff at Greenfield Community College, Amherst College, the Field Library in Conway, Historic Deerfield, the Pocumtuck Valley Memorial Society, M.N. Spear Library in Shutesbury, The Trustees of Reservations and the Carnegie Public Library in Turners Falls were particularly helpful. The area's Historical Societies, Historical Associations and Historical Commissions provided invaluable advice and access. In particular, Margaret Freeman (Hadley), Fred Goodhue and Sarah Palmer (Williamsburg), Michael Walunas (Sunderland,) Jeff Singleton (Montague), Annette Glazic (Leverett), Steve Mollison (Goshen), Jane Sabo (Deerfield), Mike Wissemann (Warner Farms) and Jack Ramey (Conway) went out of their way to provide access, information and historic images. A special thanks to Greenfield historian Peter S. Miller for his early advice on essential reference books; Dr. Alan Lutenegger of the University of Massachusetts Department of Civil and Environmental Engineering, who consulted with us on the area's rich legacy of bridges, and Timothy Neumann, Executive Director of Pocumtuck Valley Memorial Association, who provided special access to the Memorial Hall Museum's historic collections. Tony Jahn of Marshall Field's was helpful in providing an image of the company's founder. Martha Rullman undertook important contract research. Elise Engler gave us permission to use her captivating drawing of the Goshen Cemetery.

As always, my wife and daughter have supported me in this several-year effort to bring the unique attractions and beauty of another part of central western Massachusetts to a broader audience. My daughter Devon has been particularly helpful in image selection.

David J. McLaughlin

Scottsdale, Arizona

January 2006

ABOUT THE AUTHORS

David J. McLaughlin is a widely traveled writer and photographer with an abiding interest in New England. Dave was born in Boston, Massachusetts, and grew up in the central western part of the state featured in this book. He is the author of five books and over forty articles on subjects ranging from motivation to medieval history.

Laren Bright is an Emmy-nominated, award-winning writer whose diversified writing career spans more than three decades. He has written extensively for television animation, working on staff at Hanna-Barbera and Warner Bros. Animation, co-published a magazine, written dozens of articles and ghost-written three books.

ABOUT THE PHOTOGRAPHERS

Jim McElholm is the head of Single Source Inc. in Oxford, Massachusetts. Some of the images we have used are part of Jim's vast image databank, reflecting decades of New England photography. Many of the images were commissioned by Pentacle Press.

David J. McLaughlin contributed significantly to the collection of original images featured in this book. An accomplished travel photographer, Dave made seven photo trips to the area during 2003-2005. His collection of original photographs, *Images of the California Missions*, was published in 2003.

Index

A
Ashfield 76-81, 85
Ashfield Historical Society 78
Avery, James Dean 28

B
Bardwell Ferry Bridge 74–75
Barrus Farm (Goshen) 93
Bear Swamp (Ashfield) 81
Book Mill (Montague Center) 62–63
Bridge of Names (Montague Center) 65
Bub's Bar-B-Que (Sunderland) 41
Burkeville Covered Bridge (Conway) 72–73

C
Cheney, George 98
Chesterfield 90
Cole, Thomas 42–43
Connecticut River 7, 8–9, 34, 36, 42, 44, 46
Conway 66, 68–73
Cummington 82, 86–89

D
Deerfield 7, 11, 12–17, 18–29, 30, 66, 102
Deerfield Academy 14–15, 17, 26
Deerfield Inn 26, 102
Deerfield River 29
Dubuque State Memorial Forest 84

F
Field, Marshall 69-71
First Church of Deerfield (Brick Church) 23–24
Flynt, Henry N. and Helen G. 17, 19

G
Goshen 89–97
Graves, John Long 38
Greenfield 11, 16, 55, 58, 64, 102